P9-CMP-763

# Michelle Pfeiffer

Julia Holt

JAMESTOWN  PUBLISHERS

*a division of* NTC/CONTEMPORARY PUBLISHING GROUP
Lincolnwood, Illinois USA

LONGWOOD PUBLIC LIBRARY

**Acknowledgments**
Cover photo:
© Ron Davis/Shooting Star Int'l

Photos:
Page 3 © Jim Britt/Shooting Star
Page 6 © Yoram Kahana
Page 9 © S.S. Archives/Shooting Star
Page 12 & 15 © S.S./Shooting Star
Page 19 © Paramount/Shooting Star
Page 22 © Ron Davis/Shooting Star
Page 26 © Hollywood Pictures/Shooting Star


First published in United Kingdom by Hodder & Stoughton
Educational in Association with the Basic Skills Agency.

ISBN: 0-89061-420-2

Published by Jamestown Publishers,
a division of NTC/Contemporary Publishing Group, Inc.
4255 West Touhy Avenue,
Lincolnwood (Chicago), Illinois 60646–1975 U.S.A.
© 1998 by NTC/Contemporary Publishing Group, Inc.
All rights reserved. No part of this book may be reproduced, stored
in a retrieval system, or transmitted in any form or by any means
electronic, mechanical, photocopying, recording, or otherwise,
without prior permission of the publisher.
Manufactured in the United States of America.

890 VP 0 9 8 7 6 5 4 3 2 1

LONGWOOD PUBLIC LIBRARY

REAL LIVES

# Michelle Pfeiffer

## Contents

# Beginning

How does a supermarket checkout girl
get to be a top Hollywood star?

It sounds like the plot of a film.
But it's also a true story,
the story of Michelle Pfeiffer's life.

Yes, she is beautiful.
But she is also clever
and a good actress.

Michelle has made it to the top
in a man's world.
She has not counted on her looks.

She now has her own
film company with her friend, Kate.
It is called Pfeiffer-Guinzberg Productions.
She didn't move to Hollywood
until 1978 when she was 20.

As a young girl
growing up in California,
she spent more time at the beach
than she did at school.

She was a tomboy.
Her teachers called her a "wild child."

From the age of 14
she had part-time jobs.
She saved to buy
a red Mustang car
and crashed it soon after.

When she left school,
she went to work full-time
at a supermarket.

One day at the checkout
she said, "What am I doing here?"

Michelle made up her mind
to change her life.
She wanted to be an actress.

Michelle went from a supermarket checkout girl to a
Hollywood star.

Michelle found an agent
by entering beauty contests.
When she was 20,
she became Miss Orange County.
A film agent
was one of the judges.

Hollywood was the place to be.
So Michelle headed there.
Her father didn't want her to go.
He wanted her
to go back to school.

Michelle was level-headed.
She knew that she needed money.
So she kept her checkout job.
This time she worked
at the Hollywood branch
of the same supermarket.

# First Films

For a few years
she was given small parts
in TV and films.

But she was only asked
to play bimbos.
All she had to do
was stand there and be beautiful.

She didn't think she was beautiful.
She said, "I look like a duck."

Her agent was trying hard
to get her better parts.

Michelle was trying hard
to give up smoking and drinking.

Michelle with Maxwell Caulfield in *Grease 2*.

To get help with her problems,
Michelle joined
one of California's many cults.
She was with them for two years.

Luckily, in 1979,
she met Peter Horton.
He helped her
to get away from the cult.
In 1982
Peter became her first husband.

On their honeymoon
she found out
she had a part in *Grease 2*.

It was not a good film,
and it didn't make much money.
Michelle needed her strong will
to keep going.

A small part in the film *Scarface*
gave her a chance
to show she could act.

It was a violent gangster film.
Michelle played the wife
of gangster Al Pacino.

The film was a success
and so was Michelle.
One critic said,
"Most of the large cast is fine,
Michelle Pfeiffer is better."

In 1984 she had a star part
in the film *Ladyhawk.*
It was made in Italy.
This was her first trip outside the United States.

She had to be away from Peter
for five months.
This put a strain on their marriage.

In 1984 Michelle played the star role in *Ladyhawk*.

*Ladyhawk* is a love story.
The two lovers
have a curse put on them,
and they have to break it.
The film wasn't a big hit,
but the critics liked Michelle.

Back in the United States
Michelle got her first part in a comedy.
She played a jewel smuggler
in the film *Into the Night*.
The film is violent
but very funny.

Michelle found
that she was very good at comedy.
She showed confidence
and good comedy timing.

She was on her way
up the ladder.

# Working with Stars

Next, she made
three more comedy films.
One was with her husband Peter.

They loved each other,
but the marriage wasn't working.

Michelle couldn't let these problems
get in the way of her work.

Then, in 1986,
she made her most important film so far.
It was *The Witches of Eastwick*.

Michelle plays one of three women
who live in a small town.
They all have magic powers,
and they wish for a man.

Michelle with Cher and Susan Sarandon in
*The Witches of Eastwick.*

Enter Jack Nicholson playing a devil!
The women have their wish,
and they have a good time
but things go too far.
All three women become pregnant.
So they get rid of Jack Nicholson's devil
by magic.

This film gave Michelle
a chance to work
with top Hollywood stars.
She watched them and learned.
She also made good friends with Cher,
who played one of the witches.

Sadly her five year marriage finished.
It was 1987, and she was filming
*Married to the Mob.*
Michelle threw herself into work.
She and her friend Kate
went to college
to make up for the time
they lost at school.

In the same year
she also made *Tequila Sunrise*
with Mel Gibson.

She liked working with Mel
but did not like the film.
Michelle would not watch the film
when it was finished.

Her next film took her to France in 1988
and to a love affair
with an actor.
The film was *Dangerous Liaisons*.
The actor was John Malkovich.
Making this film turned out to be
a dangerous liaison in real life
for Michelle.

Michelle and John Malkovich in *Dangerous Liaisons*.

*Dangerous Liaisons*
is the story of ex-lovers.
They live in France
before the French revolution.
They play dangerous games
with the lives of others.
They use sex as a weapon.

Michelle plays a prim and proper lady.
John Malkovich plays a man who bets
he can make her sleep with him.
He does this and breaks her heart.

She dies,
and he dies in a fight with a young man
played by Keanu Reeves.

The real life love affair
between John and Michelle
came to a sad end.
He could not choose
between his wife and Michelle.
When he did choose,
she had gone back to the United States.

# Being a Star

Michelle beat Madonna
to the part of a jazz singer
in *The Fabulous Baker Boys.*
She did all her own singing
for the film.
She showed that she could do
more than comedy.

Then she made *The Russia House,*
the first film to be made in Russia
after the end of communism.
The film is a spy thriller.
It shows that there was good and bad both
inside and outside communist Russia.

Michelle was 32,
and her lover in the film
was Sean Connery.
He was 60.

She said, "Will there ever be a film
when I am 60
where I have a lover half my age?"

Back home again
Michelle had the power of a top star.
Now she could turn films down.

She turned down *Silence of the Lambs*
and *Basic Instinct*.
Would she have been right for these films?

For her next film,
she worked with Al Pacino again.
They played lovers in the film
*Frankie and Johnny.*

One scene was very difficult
for Michelle.
Scene 105 put her in a bad mood.
She had to show
her naked body to Al Pacino.

The scene took three days to film.
When it was finished,
the crew had T-shirts made
saying, "I survived scene 105!"

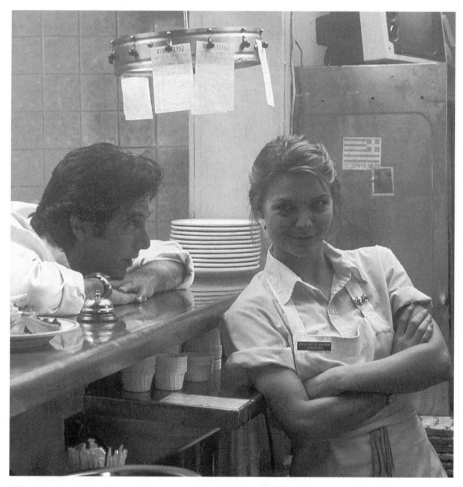

Michelle with Al Pacino in *Frankie and Johnny*.

For her next film
she had to get very fit.
It was for the part of Catwoman
in *Batman Returns*.

In the film she has to kick-box
and use a whip.
She plays a woman who changes
into the sexy Catwoman.

Michelle needed
sixty latex cat suits
to get through the film.
They were so tight
that they kept tearing.
In her house a sign turns
from "Hello There" to "Hell Here"
to show how much she has changed.

*Batman Returns*
was the top film of 1992.
It made Michelle
a star all over the world.

# Wanting a Family

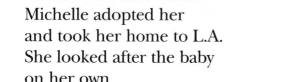

Michelle was 35,
and she wanted a more settled life.
She wanted children
so she filled in the papers
to adopt a baby.

In March 1993
Claudia Rose was born.
Michelle adopted her
and took her home to L.A.
She looked after the baby
on her own
so that they could be close.

In the same year
she met David Kelley
on a blind date.
He was to be her second husband.

He was a lawyer,
and he went on to make
the TV show *L.A. Law*.
They were married in late 1993.

Michelle with her husband David Kelley.

Now she had a family,
and the settled life she wanted.
But she wanted a baby of her own.
She said she would
only make one film a year,
so she could spend more time with her family.

In 1993
that film was *The Age of Innocence*.
It's a beautiful film
set in New York in 1870.

Michelle plays a woman
who falls in love
with her cousin's husband.
They can't be together.
What would people say?
In the end no one is happy.

For the first time
Michelle was proud of her work.
The film showed no sex or violence,
but it still made lots of money.

Her next film
was a comedy thriller.

It was called *Wolf,*
and Michelle starred
with Jack Nicholson again.
It has clever special effects
that change a middle-aged man
into a wolf.

Michelle is growing older.
She will be 40
when Claudia Rose starts school.

There are not many good film parts
for older women.
So she keeps working
while she can.

# A Wish Come True

Late in 1993 her wish came true.
She became pregnant.

The only problem was
she was in the middle of making
*Dangerous Minds.*
So in this film
she wears baggy clothes
to hide the fact
that she is pregnant.

Michelle plays a teacher
who used to be a soldier.
She teaches poor children,
and she shows them
that they can be clever.

Michelle in *Dangerous Minds*.

After the film was finished,
John Henry was born,
in August 1994.

Michelle is very happy with
her life and family.
She wanted the part of Evita,
but she chose
not to go for it.
She knows the problems
that being away from home can bring.

Instead, she chose to make
*Up Close and Personal*
with Robert Redford.

It's a romantic story
of a young waitress, played by Michelle.
She works hard
and quickly becomes a TV news reporter.
She and her boss fall in love.
Michelle's sister in the film
is played by her real sister Dee Dee.

In 1996 she starred in a film
written by her husband.
It was called *To Gillian on her 37th Birthday.*

She also showed
that she could produce films.
Michelle starred in and produced
*One Fine Day.*

It's a light-hearted film
about two single parents.
They don't like each other
when they meet.
Over the next twelve frantic hours
they change their minds.

Michelle has gone on
to produce and star in
*A Thousand Acres.*
The film was made
in 1997,
and it's about three sisters.
All three sisters
want to be their father's favorite.

She is also said
to be making
*Catwoman.*
How many latex cat suits
will she need this time?

She has come a long way
from the supermarket checkout.

If you want to see how far,
watch her films
*Up Close and Personal*
and *To Gillian on her 37th Birthday.*